World War II
The European Theatre

Edited by Phyllis Raybin Emert

 Perspectives on History

HistoryCompass
Boston, Massachusetts

HistoryCompass
www.historycompass.com

© 2005 History Compass, LLC
  2nd edition

ISBN 1-932663-12-6 paperback edition
Library of Congress Catalog Card Number 96-86714

10   9   8   7 6   5   4   3   2   1

Printed in the United States of America

Subject Reference Guide:

WORLD WAR II: The European Theatre
edited by Phyllis Raybin Emert

World War II—U.S. History

World War II—World History

Photos/Illustrations:

Photos courtesy of The National Archives and Records Administration

Credits:

Excerpts from BERLIN DIARY by William Shirer
Copyright (c) 1940, 1941 by William Shirer.
Reprinted by permission of Brandt & Brandt Literary Agents, Inc.

Excerpts from MANY KINDS OF COURAGE by Richard Lidz
Copyright (c) 1980 by Visual Education Corporation.
Reprinted by permission of The Putnam Publishing Group

Excerpts from ERNIE'S WAR - THE BEST OF ERNIE PYLE'S
WORLD WAR II DISPATCHES by Ernie Pyle
Reprinted by permission of Random House

⚔ Table of Contents ⚔

◅ Table of Contents ▻

Foreword

The widespread conflict called World War II involved every major country on earth and is considered by many historians to be the single most significant event of the twentieth century. The war affected the lives of most people throughout the world and brought about great changes in the political and economic structure of global society.

For the portion of World War II fought in Europe, this book provides a brief overview of how and why the war came about, some significant battles and military strategy, and the resolution and aftermath of the conflict. Excerpts from radio broadcasts, memoirs, interviews, diaries, newspapers, and speeches will give readers some insight into what it was like during the war years in Europe, when the fate of so many people hung in the balance.

The Road to War—How and Why?

In order to understand how and why the Second World War started, it is necessary to examine two specific historical events, namely, World War I (1914-1918) and the Great Depression that began in 1929 and lasted throughout the 1930s.

"The First War explains the Second, in fact caused it, insofar as one event explains another," declared historian A. J. P. Taylor in his book, *The Origins of the Second World War.*

In what was often called "The Great War," and later the "war to end all wars," the Central Powers of Germany and Austria-Hungary opposed the Allies, mainly England, France, Russia, and the United States (from April 1917). By the time the conflict came to an end, a revolution in Russia had overthrown the government of Czar Nicholas II and the Communist (Bolshevik) party gained control of the country (1917). In Germany, Kaiser Wilhelm abdicated and a republic was established (1918), and the Austrian-Hungarian monarchy collapsed.

The Allies were determined to prevent Germany from ever threatening world peace again. The Versailles Treaty of 1919 punished Germany severely, requiring the government to pay billions of dollars in reparations. Under its terms, the German army was reduced to a maximum of 100,000 men, the navy was limited, and the German air force, submarine, and artillery divisions were totally eliminated.

Germany had to give Alsace-Lorraine to France; the Sudetenland, to Czechoslovakia; and the Polish corridor (a strip of land that cut off East Prussia and extended to the Baltic Sea) and the free city of Danzig, to Poland. No German troops were allowed to enter the Rhineland area on Germany's western border, and Germany had to give up all its possessions overseas.

In their zeal to prevent future wars, the Allies had planted the seeds of resentment and humiliation in the German people by the harsh terms of the Versailles Treaty. Although many Germans believed the government had betrayed the people by signing what they believed to be an unjust and illegal document, Germany's new democratic government, the Weimar Republic, had no choice but to accept the conditions.

Challenged by the new left-wing communist regime in Russia, extreme nationalistic right-wing political groups took root in Europe after the war. In 1922, Benito Mussolini's fascist movement gained control of Italy, combining intense nationalism with anticommunism.

In Germany, similar right wing fanatics, fueled by the popular feeling against the Versailles Treaty, gained strength. A small group called the National Socialist German Workers Party—the Nazis—opposed the Weimar Republic. Led by a charismatic speaker named Adolf Hitler, the Nazis emphasized the need to restore Germany to world power status and to right the wrongs of the Versailles Treaty.

In November of 1923, the Nazis attempted to overthrow the government by taking some officials hostage in a beer hall where they were meeting. During this incident, referred to as the "Beer Hall Putsch," Hitler was arrested and sentenced to jail. During his imprisonment of less than a year, Hitler wrote *Mein Kampf*, which means "my struggle." In this book, part autobiography but largely a handbook for the Nazi Party, Hitler revealed his personal beliefs and plans for the future of Germany and the world.

Hitler believed in a single national leader who would have unchallenged authority. He glorified war and favored military action to provide more living space ("lebensraum") for the German people. He believed the Germans were the master race, superior to all others, and had a fanatical hatred of Jews, whom he blamed for Germany's troubles.

The Nazis remained a small political party for most of the 1920s. It was the onset of the Great Depression in 1929 that allowed them to become more powerful and influential. The German economy was still saddled with reparations payments from World War I when the Great Depression struck. Rampant inflation earlier in the 1920s had wiped out savings. The depression increased Germany's unemployment from 1.3 million people in 1929 to 6 million people in 1932.

It was Adolf Hitler who offered the people easy solutions. He blamed the nation's problems on the Jews, the democratic government, and the communists. He promised every German a job and vowed to end the reparations payments to the Allies. He promised that Germany would rise again and become a great power. In times of trouble, many people turned to these extremists who offered up scapegoats on whom to place the blame. With the use of Hitler's own private army called storm troopers, the Nazis intimidated and brutalized their political opponents. By 1930 they were the second largest party in the legislature.

Hitler ran for president against Field Marshal Paul von Hindenburg in 1932. Although Hitler lost, the Nazis received 37% of the total popular vote and gained many seats in the Reichstag (parliament). Because of the strong Nazi showing, the aged von Hindenburg, who was 84-years-old, agreed to name Hitler as Chancellor in 1933.

After the Reichstag building was burned down on February 27, 1933, Hitler blamed the communists, even though it was the Nazis themselves who had started the fire. As Chancellor, Hitler declared a state of emergency and suspended civil liberties such as freedom of speech, press, and assembly. He allowed illegal search and seizures and unwarranted arrests. He was able to strong-arm the legislature into passing laws that allowed him more and more power. By 1934, after the death of von Hindenburg, Hitler had become the absolute ruler, "der Fuehrer," and the swastika (hooked black cross) became the symbol for Nazi Germany.

In Hitler's military dictatorship, every part of a person's life was controlled by the state. Absolutely no dissent was allowed, political opponents were arrested, and their parties outlawed. The secret police, the SS, enforced Nazi rule. Jews were persecuted and imprisoned. From an early age, boys were taught to fight in the military, and girls were taught to be mothers. All children were required to join the Jungvolk and, when they were older, the Hitler Youth organizations where Nazi doctrine was taught. Books which had opposing points of view were burned, and people who appeared to be subversive disappeared in the night. Germany became a police state ruled by one man.

Having acquired complete control of Germany, Hitler turned his attention to rebuilding the military and his quest for lebensraum. Ignoring the Versailles Treaty, Hitler rearmed Germany. He rebuilt German tank divisions (panzers) and the air force (luftwaffe) and submarine (U-boat) branches of the military, all the while publicly stressing Germany's commitment to peace.

Encouraged by the world's passive attitude toward Japan's conquest of Manchuria in Northern China (1931) and Italy's seizure of Ethiopia (1936), Hitler moved two German divisions into the Rhineland in 1936. The European nations, wanting to avoid another devastating war, did nothing to stop this direct violation of the Versailles Treaty. Although a League of Nations had been established after World War I to keep the peace, no multinational force was maintained to enforce it. The League had done nothing to stop the Japanese or the Italians and did nothing to stop Hitler.

Many historians believe that a small show of force by France in 1936 would have resulted in a German retreat and the possible avoidance of the world war to come. But the French were unwilling to take a stand against Hitler and risk a conflict they wanted to avoid at all costs.

In March of 1938, confident that other European nations would do nothing to stop him, Hitler's German troops entered Austria and declared it to be a part of the German nation. Although the Austrian takeover was denounced with words by other nations, no action was taken.

Next, Hitler set his sights on the Sudetenland in Czechoslovakia and demanded its return to Germany. Hitler announced he would go to war if his demands were not met. In order to avoid a conflict, British Prime Minister Neville Chamberlain and French Premier Edouard Daladier met with Hitler in Munich. They put pressure on the Czech government to give up the Sudetenland.

Chamberlain returned to England boasting of "peace in our time," but Winston Churchill, then a member of Parliament, declared, "The belief that security can be obtained by throwing a small state to the wolves is a fatal delusion." Within a year, in March, 1939, Germany invaded and occupied the rest of Czechoslovakia without firing a shot.

This policy of giving in to Hitler's demands was called appeasement. France and Britain had hoped to satisfy Germany's demands for lebensraum and avert war. Instead, Hitler grew greedier and more confident, believing the Allies would not oppose him. Next, the Nazi dictator demanded that the Polish corridor be returned to Germany.

Joseph Stalin, the communist dictator of the Soviet Union, proposed a military alliance with France and Great Britain against Nazi Germany if Hitler should attack Poland. The offer was rejected by the Allies because Poland did not want Soviet troops within its borders even if they were there to fight the Germans.

Rebuffed by the Allies, Stalin signed a nonaggression pact with its enemy, Germany, on August 24, 1939. Hitler was now free to attack Poland without fear of Russian intervention in the East. Wasting little time, Germany invaded Poland on September 1, 1939. Two days later, France and Great Britain, followed by other British Commonwealth countries (Canada, Australia, and New Zealand) declared war on Germany. The Second World War was underway.

The following excerpts focus on statements and events leading up to World War II and what life was like in the Nazi Germany of Adolf Hitler.

Mein Kampf
by Adolf Hitler

(New York: Reynal & Hitchcock, 1940, pages 527, 964.)

FELLOW CITIZENS! Come today, Sunday, March 6, 1921, 10 a.m. to the Giant Demonstration of Protest at the Zirkus Krone

A. Hitler will speak about:

'LONDON AND US?'

White collar and manual workers of our people, you alone have to suffer the consequences of this unheard-of treaty. Come and protest against Germany being burdened with the war guilt. Protest against the peace treaty of Versailles which has been forced upon us by the sole culprit of the war, the Jewish international stock exchange capital; protest against the latest dictate from Paris; and protest finally, against a Reich's government which gives the most colossal promises without asking the German people.

Beginning of the meeting 10 a.m., end 12 noon.

Admission M. 1. – War invalids free

No Jews admitted

...Never forget that the most sacred right in this world is the right to that earth which man desires to till himself, and the most sacred sacrifice that blood which man spills for this earth...

Adolf Hitler in 1939. (Image credit: US Holocaust Memorial Museum, Washington, D.C.)

First Interview with Reich Chancellor Adolf Hitler

by H.V. Kaltenborn

(New Republic, February 15, 1933, from *They Were There – The Story of World War II and How It Came About* by *America's Foremost Correspondents,* edited by Curt Reiss. Garden City, New York: Garden City Publishing Co., 1945, page 17.)

"In America you exclude any would-be immigrants you do not care to admit," he [Hitler] said emphatically. "You regulate their number. Not content with that, you prescribe their physical condition. Not content with that, you insist on the conformity of their political opinions. We demand the same right in Germany. We have no concern with the Jews of other lands, but we are very much concerned about the anti-German elements within our country. We demand the right to deal with these elements as we see fit. Jews have been the intellectual proponents of subversive anti-German movements, and as such they must be dealt with."

Berlin Diary

by William L. Shirer

(New York: Alfred A. Knopf, 1941, pages 23, 32, 34.)

NUREMBERG, September 10, 1934—After seven days of almost ceaseless goose-stepping, speech-making, and pageantry, the party rally came to an end tonight. And though dead tired and rapidly developing a bad case of crowdphobia, I'm glad I came. You have to go through one of these to understand Hitler's hold on the people, to feel the dynamic in the movement he's unleashed and the sheer, disciplined strength the Germans possess. And now...the half-million men who've been here during the week will go back to their towns and villages and preach the new gospel with new fanaticism....

BERLIN, March 17, 1935—...Hitler and his henchmen were in the royal box, but he himself did not speak. General von Blomberg spoke for him, though it seemed to me that he was uttering words certainly penned by the Fuhrer. Said Blomberg: "The world has been made to realize that Germany did not die of its defeat in the World

War. Germany will again take the place she deserves among the nations. We pledge ourselves to a Germany which will never surrender and never again sign a treaty which cannot be fulfilled. We do not need revenge because we have gathered glory enough through the centuries."

...Finally [Hitler's proclamation] to Germans and the whole world:

" ...In this hour the German government renews before the German people and before the entire world its assurance of its determination never to proceed beyond the safeguarding of German honour and the freedom of the Reich [the German empire and government], and especially it does not intend in rearming Germany to create any instrument for warlike attack, but, on the contrary, exclusively for defense and thereby for the maintenance of peace...."

★★★

Howl Like the Wolves – Growing up in Nazi Germany
by Max Von Der Grun

(New York: William Morrow and Company, 1980, pp 104-105.)

Citizenship Law of September 15, 1935

Article 1
(1). No one can be a citizen unless he belongs to the defensive league of the German Reich and, for this reason, is under particular obligation to it....

Article 2
(1). No one can be a citizen of the Reich unless he is a citizen of German blood or German-related stock, whose conduct proves that he is willing and able to serve faithfully the German people and the German Reich....

Law to Protect German Blood and German Honor, enacted on September 15, 1935

Article 1

(1). Marriages between Jews and citizens of German blood or German-related stock are forbidden. Any marriages entered into in violation of this law are invalid, even if, in order to evade this law, the couple are married abroad....

Article 2

Extramarital [relations] between Jews and citizens of German blood or German-related stock is forbidden....

Article 5

(1). Anyone who violates the prohibition of Article 1 will be sentenced to prison....

(2). A man who violates the prohibition of Article 2 will be sentenced to jail or prison....

☆☆☆

Account of Kurt Lange, German Citizen

(Lidz, Richard. *Many Kinds of Courage.* NewYork: G. P. Putnam' s Sons, 1980, page 23.)

It had become clear back in early 1936 that the Nazi movement could do whatever it pleased. It was then that Hitler had marched into the demilitarized zone of the Rhineland with his troops, and nobody had moved against him....This was actually the clearest sign to the Nazi movement that they could do what they pleased, because the world would not intervene. This was a moment when, within a day, the marching of French troops into the Rhineland would have put an end to Hitler's power then and there. But nothing happened.

Cowardice is the guiding word for the origin of the Hitler movement. Whether it was the German democratic groups, or whether it was the Allies who didn't realize what was going on, no one was prepared to stand up to the Nazis. But this could have been done, because at that time it was a fragile, noisy...movement which did not actually have the strength to fight. Had he been prevented from reoccupying the Rhineland, Hitler's power would have been ended.

Memoirs of the Second World War

by Winston S. Churchill

(Cambridge, Massachusetts: Houghton Mifflin Company - The Riverside Press, 1959, pages 105-106.)

One day in 1937 I had a meeting with Herr von Ribbentrop German Ambassador to Britain ....The gist of his statement to me was that...Britain should give Germany a free hand in the East of Europe. She must have her Lebensraum, or living space, for her increasing population....All that was asked of the British Commonwealth and Empire was not to interfere....

After hearing all this I said at once that I was sure the British Government would not agree to give Germany a free hand in Eastern Europe....He then said, "In that case, war is inevitable. There is no way out. The Fuehrer is resolved. Nothing will stop him and nothing will stop us...." [Churchill replied] "Do not underrate England. She is very clever. If you plunge us all into another Great War she will bring the whole world against you, like last time." At this the Ambassador rose in heat and said, "Ah England may be very clever, but this time she will not bring the world against Germany."

★★★

Adolf Hitler To Austrian Chancellor, Herr von Schuschnigg

February 12, 1938

(Churchill, page 119, taken from *Schuschnigg, Ein Requiem in Rot-Weiss-Rot*, page 37.)

...Don't believe that anyone in the world will hinder me in my decisions! Italy? I am quite clear with Mussolini: with Italy I am on the closest possible terms. England? England will not lift a finger for Austria...And France? Well, two years ago when we marched into the Rhineland with a handful of battalions—at that moment I risked a great deal. If France had marched then we should have been forced to withdraw....But for France it is now too late!

Speech by Adolf Hitler in Reichenberg, Germany
December 2, 1938

(from Von Der Grun *op. cit.*, pages 118-119.)

These young people will learn nothing else but how to think German and act German. And when, at the age of ten, this boy and this girl enter our organizations and there, frequently for the first time in their lives, breathe and feel a breath of fresh air, then four years later they will leave the Jungvolk to enter the Hitler Youth, and once again we will keep them there for four years; and then, instead of returning them to the hands of those adults who created our old social classes and ranks, we will immediately admit them into the Party or put them in the National Socialist Labor Front, the SA (stormtroopers), or the SS (protection squads - secret police), in the National Socialist Motor Corps, and so on. And if they remain there for two years or for a year and a half and have not yet become totally dedicated National Socialists, then they will be sent to work in the Labor Service and will be polished there for six or seven months.... And if any remnants of class consciousness or the arrogance of rank is left in them after six or seven months there, they will be turned over to the Armed Forces to undergo an additional two years' treatment....And they will never be free again, not their whole lives long.

Kurt Lange
(from Lidz, *op cit.*, pages 18, 19, 20, 28.)

If anybody tries to find out whether people can be brainwashed, they don't need to do any experiments because the example is already there. The German nation was brainwashed. Systematically, continuously, without recourse to any other information....Virtually everybody believed the junk that came over the radio, even up to the very end....

In the beginning, the response to the Nazi movement was not very furious in most circles. For many years, even under Hitler, everybody had the idea that this spoof was soon going to be over. Initially, nobody took him very seriously....

It is difficult in retrospect to understand how we could have continued to delude ourselves, although those who went through the time will remember that this gradual disappearance of the floor on which you are standing was not like falling into a big hole. It was rather a slow sinking which you always hoped would stop—that you would find a way out....

Those were unbelievable times. Only someone who was there and went through the anxieties of daily living can imagine the courage that one had to develop in order to overcome the most impossible situations....

Sudenten woman, forced to salute Hitler

Blitzkrieg over Europe

The German military advance into Poland was so swift and overwhelming that the French and English did not have time to mobilize their forces and enter the conflict. After less than five weeks, Poland surrendered to the German blitzkrieg (lightning war).

This new type of warfare was distinguished by fast-moving panzer attacks on the ground and frightening air attacks by black gull-winged Stuka dive bombers with sirens attached to their wings. Within days after Poland's surrender, the Russians and Germans had divided the country between them.

At this time a lull in the fighting occurred called the "phony war." France and Britain prepared for the conflict they knew was to come, while Hitler planned his next offensive against the west. Finally on April 9, 1940, Germany invaded Denmark and Norway, and, on May 10, moved against Belgium, Luxembourg, and the Netherlands.

France and Britain were certain a German attack would soon come through the Maginot Line, a 250-mile-long series of fortifications that the French had built on the German border to protect themselves from aggressors. It was here the Allied troops were massed. But in a surprise move, the Germans moved rapidly across Belgium and through the Ardennes Forest, around the Maginot Line and directly into France. Allied troops were unprepared for the Nazi blitzkrieg. The Germans crushed all opposition and moved quickly to cut off and surround French and British soldiers.

Winston Churchill, British prime minister as of May 10, 1940, had no option but to evacuate British forces from the Port of Dunkerque (also spelled Dunkirk) on the western coast of Northern France. In ten days, the English evacuated over 300,000 allied soldiers using any vessel that could cross the Channel and bring the men back to England (a distance of 20 miles at its shortest point). All available military vessels were used in the rescue effort as well as fishing barges, boats, and even civilian pleasure craft. Although it was a military defeat, the people were so united by the successful British evacuation effort that it became a worldwide symbol of resistance against the Nazis.

With the official surrender of France on June 22, 1940, Hitler was now the master of Europe, though not of Great Britain, which stood alone against the Nazi onslaught.

With the signing of an Italian/German alliance in 1936, the term "Axis" was used to refer to the major fascist powers. Italy entered the war in June 1940 on Germany's side and attacked British forces in North Africa in September and Greece in October.

The Japanese officially joined the Axis powers when all three signed the Tripartite Pact in September 1940. The militaristic regimes of Germany, Italy, and Japan had similar goals: all wanted to expand their territory and power at the expense of their neighbors.

The Japanese occupied French Indochina after the fall of France, prompting the United States and Great Britain to end the export of raw materials to Japan and to freeze Japanese assets. Relations with the western powers deteriorated and the empire of Japan secretly prepared for war against the United States.

Many Americans were isolationists and opposed any involvement in foreign conflicts. Officially, America was neutral in the European war. Still, President Franklin D. Roosevelt believed it was only a matter of time before the U.S. would also be involved in this global conflict.

In 1940, in support of America's British allies, Roosevelt signed an executive order trading 50 U.S. destroyers to England in exchange for English naval and air bases. The Lend Lease Act of March 1941 allowed the United States to lend weapons to those countries fighting the Nazis. Thus, America became the "great arsenal of democracy," according to Roosevelt, without actual U.S. military involvement.

Although Hitler offered terms of surrender to Great Britain, the English refused to even consider the possibility. "Let us therefore brace ourselves to our duties," said Churchill to the House of Commons, "and so bear ourselves that if the British Empire and its Commonwealth last for a thousand years men will say: 'this was their finest hour.' "

Night after night, beginning in July 1940, the British were attacked by waves of German dive bombers and fighter planes. This air offensive was in preparation for a German invasion of Great Britain, but the Luftwaffe never anticipated the strength and courage of the RAF (Royal Air Force) pilots and the British people. Using the new science of radar to their advantage, the RAF had advance warning of air attacks and managed to hold their own against the German planes.

On August 22, 1940, after the Luftwaffe bombed London, Britain retaliated with an air raid on Berlin. Although little damage was inflicted, this attack on the Nazi capital hurt German morale as well as Hitler's ego. The angry Fuhrer ordered the Luftwaffe to stop attacking British airfields and begin bombing London and other British cities. Many historians believe the Luftwaffe could have destroyed the RAF if Hitler had not changed his tactics. The beginning of the bombing of London (called the "blitz") allowed the British time to rebuild their airfields and build new fighter planes and bombers.

Beginning in September 1940, German planes attacked London for 57 consecutive nights. Thousands of British children were evacuated to the countryside for their safety. Although 30,000 civilians died in the blitz, the English were more determined than ever to resist the German onslaught.

As the days passed, British morale remained high and RAF bombers and fighter planes continued to attack German targets. It soon became clear to Hitler that the British would not be defeated in the air or on the ground. The Battle of Britain was Hitler's first major defeat of the war, and Hitler's plan to invade Britain was postponed indefinitely.

The Fuehrer now turned his attention to Soviet Russia. On June 22, 1941, breaking the nonaggression pact of 1939, Hitler surprised the world by attacking his former ally and extending the war to two fronts. In the west, Germany continued its attacks on Great Britain, while in the east the Russians felt the full effects of the Nazi blitzkrieg as the Germans invaded their homeland. The Nazis never anticipated the fierce resistance of the Russian people, nor did the lightly-clad German troops, who began their offensive in the summer, expect to face the bitterly cold Russian winter.

Great Britain and Russia were now allies in the fight against Nazi Germany, and it was only a matter of months before the United States would enter the global conflict.

The following excerpts focus on the early part of the war, including the fall of France and the Battle of Britain.

Speech to Parliament, June 4, 1940

by Winston S. Churchill

(from Churchill, *op cit*., pages 284-285.)

Even though large tracts of Europe and many old and famous States have fallen or may fall into the grip of the Gestapo and all the odious apparatus of Nazi rule, we shall not flag or fail. We shall go on to the end. We shall fight in France, we shall fight in the seas and oceans, we shall fight with growing confidence and growing strength in the air; we shall defend our Island, whatever the cost may be. We shall fight on the beaches, we shall fight on the landing-grounds, we shall fight in the fields and in the streets, we shall fight in the hills; we shall never surrender; and even if, which I do not for a moment believe, this island or a large part of it were subjugated and starving, then our Empire beyond the seas, armed and guarded by the British Fleet, would carry on the struggle, until, in God's good time, the New World, with all its power and might, steps forth to the rescue and the liberation of the old.

Prime Minister Winston Churchill, President Franklin D. Roosevelt, and Premier Josef Stalin. The "Big Three" at the Yalta conference in 1945.

Berlin Diary
by William L. Shirer

(Shirer, *op cit*, pages 403-405, 419.)

BERLIN, June 14, 1940—Paris has fallen. The hooked-cross flag of Hitler flutters from the Eiffel Tower there by the Seine in that Paris which I knew so intimately and loved....Poor Paris! I weep for her. For so many years it was my home—and I love it as you love a woman....I do not want to see the heavy-heeled German boots tramping down the streets I loved.

PARIS, June 21, 1940—On the exact spot in the little clearing in the Forest of Compiegne where at five a.m. on November 11, 1918 the armistice which ended the World War was signed, Adolf Hitler today handed his armistice terms to France. To make German revenge complete, the meeting of the German and French plenipotentiaries [agents authorized to represent their governments] took place in Marshal Foch's private car, in which Foch laid down the armistice terms to Germany twenty-two years ago. Even the same table in the rickety old wagon-lit car was used. And through the windows we saw Hitler occupying the very seat on which Foch had sat at that table when he dictated the other armistice.

The humiliation of France, of the French, was complete. And yet in the preamble to the armistice terms Hitler told the French that he had not chosen this spot at Compiegne out of revenge; merely to right an old wrong. From the demeanour of the French delegates I gathered that they did not appreciate the difference.

Appeal by General De Gaulle to the French
June 18, 1940

(De Gaulle, Charles. *War Memoirs - The Call to Honour 1940-1942*. New York: The Viking Press, 1955. pages 83-84.)

...I ask you to believe me when I say that the cause of France is not lost. The very factors that brought about our defeat may one day lead us to victory....

I, General De Gaulle, now in London, call on all French officers and men who are at present on British soil, or may be in the future, with or without their arms; I call on all engineers and skilled workmen from the armaments factories who are at present on British soil, or may be in the future, to get in touch with me.

Whatever happens, the flame of French resistance must not and shall not die.

★★★

This is London
by Edward R. Murrow

(New York: Simon and Schuster, 1941, pages 162-163.)

SEPTEMBER 10, 1940, 6:45 P.M.

...We are told today that the Germans believe Londoners, after a while, will rise up and demand a new government, one that will make peace with Germany. It's more probably that they'll rise up and murder a few German pilots who come down by parachute. The life of a parachutist would not be worth much in the East End of London tonight.

The politicians who called this a "people's war" were right, probably more right than they knew at the time. I've seen some horrible sights in this city during these days and nights, but not once have I heard man, woman, or child suggest that Britain should throw in her hand. These people are angry. How much they can stand, I don't know. The strain is very great....

★★★

English Poster

(Poster, from Robert Westall, Children of the Blitz - Memoirs of Wartime Childhood. New York: Viking, 1985, page 86.)

> **HITLER WILL SEND NO WARNING**
> **so always carry your gas mask**

Coventry Shattered

by Alfred Wall

(Associated Press, Nov. 15, 1940.)

COVENTRY, ENGLAND, November 15—German bombers have blasted the heart out of this once peaceful city in the English midlands with a dusk-to-dawn raid which turned parts of the city into an inferno and left at least 1,000 dead and injured.

Coventry's beautiful and famous brownstone cathedral is a smoking wreck. Only its big main spire, 303 feet high, remains standing. All the rest of the medieval structure, started in 1373 and completed in 1450, lies in a tangle of broken stone and crumpled debris....

The town was like a scene out of Hades between dusk and dawn while German raiders dumped their bombs in ceaseless relays.

A full moon shone last night, but its brilliance was dimmed by a pall of smoke and the glare of fire from burning buildings.

Scarcely a street escaped the pounding of the raiders. It was the worst continuous attack experienced by any city—including London—since the siege of Britain began.

All night long, the narrow streets where Lady Godiva rode on her horse nearly 1,000 years ago trembled and crumbled with the thunder of diving planes, the screams of bombs and their explosions and the roar of anti-aircraft cannonade....

Royal Air Force pilots took fire hoses from the hands of firemen reeling with fatigue, and played streams of water on the smoldering heaps of rubble which are all that remain of some of Britain's finest examples of Tudor architecture.

Ernie's War - The Best of Ernie Pyle's World War II Dispatches

Great Britain: December 1940 - March 1941
by Ernie Pyle

(New York: Random House, 1986, pages 52-53.)

LONDON, January 29, 1941—I got my very first view of an underground shelter crowd at the big Liverpool Street tube [subway] station. It was around eight o'clock on a raidless night. A policeman in the upper vestibule told us just to go down the escalator and take a look—as though it were a zoo. So we did.

Somehow I must have thought that there'd be nobody down there that night, or that if there were they'd be invisible or something, because I wasn't emotionally ready at all to see people lying around by the thousands on cold concrete....

On benches on each side, as though sitting and lying on a long streetcar seat, were the people, hundreds of them. And as we walked they stretched into thousands.

In addition, there was a row of sleeping forms on the wooden floor of the tube, stretched crosswise. Their bodies took up the whole space, so we had to watch closely when we put our feet down between the sleepers.

Many of these people were old—wretched and worn old people, people who had never known many of the good things of life and who were now winding up their days on this earth in desperate discomfort.

They were the bundled-up, patched-up people with lined faces that we have seen for years sitting dumbly in waiting lines at our own relief offices at home.

There were children too, some asleep and some playing. There were youngsters in groups, laughing and talking and even singing.

There were smart-alecks and there were quiet ones. There were hard-working people of middle age who had to rise at five and go to work.

Some people sat knitting or playing cards or talking. But mostly they just sat. And though it was only eight o'clock, many of the old people were already asleep.

Tube Station being used as a bomb shelter in October 1940

It was the old people who seemed so tragic. Think of yourself at seventy or eighty, full of pain and the dim memories of a lifetime that has probably all been bleak. And then think of yourself now, traveling at dusk every night to a subway station, wrapping your ragged overcoat about your old shoulders and sitting on a wooden bench with your back against a curved steel wall. Sitting there all night, in nodding and fitful sleep.

Think of that as your destiny—every night, every night from now on....

America Joins the Fight

It was inevitable that the United States and Germany would clash in the North Atlantic's shipping lanes. German U-boats attempted to blockade Great Britain at the same time American ships carried weapons of war and other supplies to the allied powers.

The merchant ship *Robin Moor* was the first American vessel to be sunk by Germany on May 21, 1941. After a battle between the *USS Greer* and a German U-boat (in which neither vessel was sunk), President Roosevelt issued a "shoot on sight" order to American ships.

In October, 1941, the *USS Kearny* was torpedoed and two weeks later the U.S. destroyer *Reuben James* was sunk. Some Americans demanded an immediate declaration of war on Nazi Germany, but isolationist thought was still strong, and the President refrained from taking any action.

As 1941 came to a close, the Japanese believed the United States was the main obstacle to their plans for a Pacific empire. Early on the morning of December 7, Japanese fighter planes, without warning, attacked the American fleet at Pearl Harbor, Hawaii, as well as in the Philippines, Malaya, Hong Kong, Wake Island, Midway, and Guam.

The United States, followed by Great Britain, declared war on the empire of Japan on December 8. In support of their Axis partner, both Germany and Italy honored the Tripartite Pact by declaring war on the United States on December 11.

Now faced with a war in Europe and the Pacific, Roosevelt and Churchill decided that the defeat of Germany would be their nations' top priority. In Europe, the U.S. Eighth Air Force joined the RAF in bombing missions over occupied France and later over Germany. The first important Allied victory came in October 1942 when Britain's 8th Army under General Bernard Montgomery drove German Field Marshal Irwin Rommel's Afrika Korps out of El Alamein in Egypt. It was a major defeat for Germany.

The following month (November, 1942) brought the successful Allied invasion of North Africa under American General Dwight D. Eisenhower, in which 85,000 American and 23,000 British troops landed in French Morocco and Algeria. It was not until May of 1943, after six months of hard desert warfare, that the Germans and Italians were finally driven out of Africa.

Meanwhile, the Soviet Union, with the help of Allied supplies, managed to hold off the Germans in 1942 but at the price of widespread death and destruction in their homeland. After rapidly advancing deep into Soviet territory, the Germans were finally stalled by the combination of the severe Russian winter and the desperate fighting of the Russian troops. Finally, in the summer of '42, the German armies and panzer divisions were ordered by Hitler to begin a major offensive against the city of Stalingrad.

The battle of Stalingrad was the turning point of the war in Europe and among the bloodiest ever fought. The Soviets were determined to hold the city at all costs. It was a fierce and brutal struggle often resulting in hand-to-hand combat from house-to-house and street-to-street.

The battle for Stalingrad lasted 80 days, allowing the Soviets time to gather reserve forces and encircle the German Sixth Army. The Germans finally surrendered on January 31, 1943, giving the Russians their first victory of the war. More than a million Soviet and German troops were killed in the battle, and Stalingrad lay in ruins.

Along with the British victory at El Alamein, the outcome at Stalingrad convinced the Allies that Nazi Germany would eventually be defeated. The remainder of the war was dominated by a U.S. arsenal that produced countless weapons to supply Allied troops throughout the world.

The following excerpts focus on the effect of America's entry into the war, the Allied offensive in North Africa, the air war in Europe, and the battle of Stalingrad.

Memoirs of the Second World War

by Winston S. Churchill

(from Churchill, *op cit.*, pages 506-507.)

No American will think it wrong of me if I proclaim that to have the United States at our side was to me the greatest joy. I could not foretell the course of events. I do not pretend to have measured accurately the martial might of Japan, but now at this very moment I knew the United States was in the war, up to the neck and in to the death. So we had won after all! Yes, after Dunkirk; after the fall of France...after the threat of invasion, when, apart from the Air and the Navy, we were an almost unarmed people; after the deadly struggle of the U-boat war...after seventeen months of lonely fighting and nineteen months of my responsibility in dire stress. We had won the war. England would live....We should not be wiped out. Our history would not come to an end....No doubt it would take a long time. I expected terrible forfeits in the East; but all this would be merely a passing phase. United we could subdue everybody else in the world. Many disasters, immeasurable cost and tribulation lay ahead, but there was no more doubt about the end.

Silly people, and there were many, not only in enemy countries, might discount the force of the United States. Some said they were soft, others that they would never be united. They would fool around at a distance. They would never come to grips. They would never stand bloodletting. Their democracy and system of recurrent elections would paralyze their war effort. They would be just a vague blur on the horizon to friend or foe. Now we should see the weakness of this numerous but remote, wealthy, and talkative people. But I had studied the American Civil War, fought out to the last desperate inch. American blood flowed in my veins. I thought of a remark which Edward Grey had made to me more than thirty years before—that the United States is like "a gigantic boiler. Once the fire is lighted under it there is no limit to the power it can generate...."

El Alamein—Push Begins in Mighty Barrage

by Richard D. Macmillan

(*The New York Times*, Oct. 26, 1942.)

INSIDE THE GERMAN LINES, on the Egyptian Front, Oct. 24 (Delayed)—The biggest battle of Egypt is under way.

The British have attacked violently and have penetrated the enemy positions at many points. Tanks are passing in strength through gaps in the minefields.

The heaviest fighting is inside the German lines, and I am with the Fifty-first Highland Division, which burst through the German outer defenses.

The British have already advanced well into the enemy sector at some points, although many were held up in others, and fighting of the heaviest kind, involving both infantry and tanks, is going on.

This offensive began with the speed of lightning.

An Air Transport Command Plane, loaded with supplies from the U.S., flies over the pyramids of Egypt in 1943.

A skirl of bagpipes resounded from the Highlanders' front positions last night and the sound of music in the chill, moonlit desert must have been clearly audible in the German front lines, a few hundred yards away.

Suddenly the music was drowned out by the greatest blast of guns ever heard in Egypt.

The Allied barrage had opened with a terrifying roar from hundreds of guns. The battle was on....

The first burst of guns soon gave way to a deafening clamor from hundreds of tanks rumbling out of hiding places in dry water courses. The tanks churned up a sandstorm as they raced into battle on our right, left and center. They pushed up to the enemy lines under a monstrous flaring and blaring of artillery and rode roughshod over the startled German African Corps....

★★★

Bombing of Cologne
by Robert E. Bunnelle

(Associated Press, May 30, 1942.)

...Already the sky was filled with [the] roar of planes from the other fields, all getting ready for the 1,250-bomber party at Cologne—the world's first four-figure air raid....

"How much longer before we're there, navigator?"

"About ten minutes," replied the navigator.

"Well, we don't need you anymore. That light's Cologne. The fellows have built up quite a fire."

By this time the sky became so full of flak, tracers, shell bursts, and spotlight streaks that it was like the fireworks at the county fair. The Germans were throwing everything they had at the attackers. From the bomb aimer's hatch, Cologne glowed like a big cigarette end in a blackout. Then the plane was directly over the fires and the captain ordered: "Bomb doors open!"

"Bomb doors open," came the reply.

The captain spoke again. He said: "Hell, wait a minute. No use wasting stuff on burning buildings. Let's look for a black spot."

Block after block of the town was blazing under the craft, smoke drifting past the flame-outlined wings. In the blaze could be seen what appeared to be white-hot skeletons of steel framework.

There were Wellingtons, Halifaxes, Manchesters, [British bombers] more Stirlings—in fact, about everything but helicopters—flying above, below, and on either side of the Stirling. All were silhouetted against the towering flames of Cologne. And all were dropping their loads on Cologne....

One tiny dark spot showed on the Rhine river's flowing west bank.

"That might be Elektra Stahldraht Fabrik [a steel wire plant]," said the captain. "Let's try it."

There followed an anxious moment of leveling off and moving right and left to get on the target. Then the bomb aimer pressed the button and the plane gave a lift from the release of the heavy bomb cargo....The ship slipped through the flak and the rear gunner shouted, "We got it! I saw the white flash of debris flying, then red and yellow flames shooting up."

There were shouts of elation on the ship's phone! The job had been done. The Stirling's bombs had found their mark. The Stirling skirted the city, setting a homeward course. The burning area had increased tremendously in the eight minutes over the target. New fires were springing up everywhere. About ninety miles from Cologne, the captain turned in a complete circle to take another look. From this distance, the three major fires had merged into one immense volcano of flame.

The Stirling dodged and spiraled on to England, trying to confuse Nazi night fighters and ground observers....

At a United States Flying Fortress Base in England

by Walter Cronkite, United Press

(*The New York Times*, February 27, 1943.)

Saturday, Feb. 27 (UP)—American Flying Fortresses have just come back from an assignment to hell—a hell 26,000 feet above the earth, a hell of burning tracer bullets and bursting gunfire, of crippled Fortresses and burning German fighter planes, of parachuting men and others not so lucky. I have just returned with a Flying Fortress crew from Wilhelmshaven [Germany].

We fought off Hitler's fighters and dodged his guns. The Fortress I rode in came out without damage, but we had the element of luck on our side.

Other formations caught the blast of fighter blows and we watched Fortresses and Liberators plucked out of the formations around us.

We gave the ship repair yards and other installations at the great German submarine and naval base of the North Sea a most severe pasting. As we swept beyond the target and back over the North Sea from which we came we saw great pillars of smoke over the target area....

Actually, the impressions of a first bombing mission are a hodge-podge of disconnected scenes like a poorly edited home movie— bombs falling past you from the formation above, a crippled bomber with smoke pouring from one motor limping along thousands of feet below, a tiny speck in the sky that grows closer and finally becomes an enemy fighter, a Focke-Wulf [German fighter] peeling off above you somewhere and plummeting down, shooting its way through the formation; your bombardier pushing a button as calmly as if he were turning on a hall light, to send our bombs on the way.

...the bomb bay doors swing open on the lead ship on down the line to us.

That signaled that we were beginning the bomb run. Then we swept over Wilhelmshaven. There were broken clouds but through them there appeared a toy village below which was really a major seaport and I thought:

"Down there right now people are scurrying for shelters—which means interrupting work on vital submarines and ships and dock yards."...

"Bombs away."

That was it. Our mission was accomplished—our bombs were on their way to Hitler.

★★★

The Inglorious Finale of the Nazi Adventure
by Roman Karmen

(Soviet Army correspondents, *The Epic Story of Stalingrad*. Hutchinson & Co., Ltd., no date or place, from *Masterpieces of War Reporting*, Louis L. Snyder, editor. New York: Julian Messner, Inc. 1962, pages 229, 232-233.)

...The city was nearly cleared of the enemy. Only two nests remained where Germans were still offering futile resistance. Step by step, quarter by quarter, our troops were mopping up in Stalingrad, smoking the Germans out of the houses by artillery fire or digging them out at the point of the bayonet, and after each such drive hundreds and more hundreds of enemy soldiers would give themselves up....

As one walks along the streets and squares of this great and beautiful city destroyed by Hitler, which will now have to be entirely rebuilt, one feels one would like to bare one's head silently in front of these noble ruins, whose every stone, every fragment of it, is stained with the blood of our warriors and bears witness to the glory of the Soviet people. The accurate German strategists took everything into account. But in their variegated military terminology they forgot one word and its meaning: they forgot the word "Russia," and they met their death among the ruins of the city which has become the symbol of the stubborn strength of our country.

We will build you up again, you great city of Stalingrad! Inspired architects, painters and sculptors will create buildings of marble and granite and lay out green squares and parks. Our factories will be rebuilt. But mankind will never forget these ruins, nor the Soviet heroes who fought to the last throb of their hearts on staircases, behind smoking heaps of stones, in cellars and back alleys and held their city.

The Invasion of Italy

After the Allied victory in North Africa, a decision was made to invade Sicily and Italy in 1943. The goal was to get at Hitler through what Churchill referred to as the "soft underbelly" of Europe. A full-scale invasion of France, opening up a second front in Europe (in addition to the Russian's eastern front) was postponed until 1944.

The U.S. 7th Army under General George S. Patton, Jr. and the British 8th Army under General Montgomery succeeded in conquering Sicily (an island off the southwestern Italian coast) in five weeks. After the Sicilian offensive, the low morale and wavering loyalty of the Italian troops helped bring about the overthrow of Benito Mussolini. The Italian people were not happy with the war, and members of Mussolini's own cabinet arrested and imprisoned the fascist leader.

On September 2, 1943, more than 70,000 American troops under General Mark Clark landed at Salerno Beach on the mainland of Italy, south of Rome. The following day, September 3, the new Italian government signed a peace treaty with the Allies. If the Italians thought they could avoid war, they were mistaken. In order to meet the new Allied offensive, the Germans moved large numbers of troops into Italy to meet the American threat. Clark hoped to take Salerno and then Naples within a week. But the German defenders put up such a furious fight that it was weeks before the Americans advanced beyond Salerno and joined up with the British 8th Army under Montgomery. It was not until early October that the combined Allied forces took Naples.

The so-called soft underbelly of the Axis turned out to be one of the most difficult campaigns of the war. The rugged and mountainous Italian terrain was impassable to tanks, and in places where trucks could not go, the infantrymen used mules to carry supplies. The march to take Rome was a brutal and bloody ground struggle from ridge to ridge and hill to hill, and it was the foot soldier who endured the harsh realities of day-to-day combat. As 1943 ended, progress in Italy had slowed and some Allied troops were withdrawn and sent to England in preparation for the upcoming invasion of France.

In an effort to break through the German defenses, called the Gustav Line, a British-American force of 50,000 landed at Anzio, thirty miles south of Rome, on January 22, 1944. For months, the Allies, encircled by Germans, could not break out of Anzio and suffered heavy casualties. Further south, other Allied forces tried and failed to capture the town of Cassino, even after continuous bombing and artillery attacks. It was not until May 11, nearly four months later, that 50,000 men of the Polish Army, fighting with the Allies, captured Cassino, and on May 23 that the Americans broke out of Anzio.

American troops fire a 155 mm
"Long Tom" gun in Italy

The German troops retreated northward, and General Mark Clark marched into Rome on June 4, 1944. Within days of the capture of Rome, the Italian campaign took a back seat to the invasion of France and the second front in Europe.

Meanwhile, the air offensive against Germany in 1943 and 1944 had developed into round-the-clock bombing of the heart of the Nazi empire. The RAF engaged in night bombing of German cities and outlying areas, while the American air forces, using the new Norden bombsight, with greater accuracy, preferred daylight bombing from higher altitudes.

With the conquest of southern Italy in 1944, Allied bomber attacks began to originate from Italian airbases as well as from England. The Luftwaffe had to cope with air attacks from the west as well as the south. By this time, the newest and deadliest American fighter plane, the P-51 Mustang, was accompanying U.S. bombers on raids into Germany and proved to be superior to any German fighter plane encountered in combat.

Allied bombers concentrated on destroying enemy factories, weapons facilities, U-boat plants, and oil refineries. Their goal was to achieve air superiority over Europe before the Allied invasion of France.

As the air war heated up, so did the battle of the Atlantic. Whereas German U-boats enjoyed dominance in the early years of the war, Allied submarine strength increased substantially by mid-1943, meeting and overcoming the German U-boat threat. This resulted in a dramatic decrease in Allied merchant shipping losses to German naval forces in 1943 and 1944.

The following excerpts focus on the invasion of Italy and the air war in Europe.

The Front Line in Italy

Italy: December 1943 - May 1944
by Ernie Pyle

(from Pyle, *op cit.*, pages 172-173, 194.)

AT THE FRONT LINE IN ITALY, December 14, 1943—The war in Italy is tough. The land and the weather are both against us.

It rains and it rains. Vehicles bog down and temporary bridges wash out. The country is shockingly beautiful, and just as shockingly hard to capture from the enemy. The hills rise to high ridges of almost solid rock. You can't go around them through the flat peaceful valleys, because the Germans look down upon you and would let you have it....

January 8, 1944—...The fighting on the mountain-top sometimes almost reaches the caveman stage. The Americans and Germans are frequently so close that they actually throw rocks at each other.

They use up many times as many hand grenades as we have had in any other phase of the Mediterranean war. And you have to be pretty close when you throw hand grenades.

Rocks play a big part in the mountain war. You hide behind rocks, you throw rocks, you sleep in rock crevices, and you even get killed by flying rocks.

Also, now and then an artillery burst from a steep hillside will loosen big boulders which go leaping and bounding down the mountainside for thousands of yards. The boys say such a rock sounds like a windstorm coming down the mountainside....

Serenade to the Big Bird

by Bert Stiles

(*I Have Seen War*, Dorothy Sterling, editor. New York: Hill and Wang, 1960, pages 68 - 73.)

...We started our engines at six o'clock. They kicked over right on down the line...start one, mesh one...start two...mesh two...good engines...

Grant gave me the heading over the interphone and we started climbing on course, away from the blood-colored dawn.

Sam and I had decided to trade off every fifteen minutes until we got used to going to war, but he flew most of the assembly, and I just changed the r.p.m. when he called for it and sweated.

I thought the eighteen planes would never get together. We just flew around and around, getting nowhere, and then miraculously we were all in, flying off the right leaders, trying to look pretty.

We formed at seventeen thousand and my oxygen mask was bothering me, and my hair was soupy with sweat, and I couldn't move my shoulders in my electric suit. It was too late to do anything though....

We flew up across the Channel and cut in at the Dutch coast. The navigator was on the ball, and we didn't see any flak until we were out in the Zuider Zee. Some other wing navigator was asleep and they caught it right in the middle of the formation. Nobody went down. Pretty black puffs in a blue sky...harmless looking stuff....

"We're over the Third Reich," Benson announced.

The land was all chopped up into little fields and little towns. The fields were just as green as England, greener than Illinois when we crossed it last. They used the same sun down there, and the same moon. The sky was just as blue to them as to anyone at home probably. But for some reason the people down there were Nazis....

I didn't have any idea we were near the target until I saw the lead ship's bomb bays swing open....

The bombs fell out of the lead ship and Bird yelled ours were gone....

Everyone was letting down a thousand feet so we could get out of the country a little sooner. A couple of wings off to the left were catching some flak and somebody had wiped out most of a town down to our right. We seemed to be out on the edge of the show.

"We're in France now," Benson called up....

I couldn't tell the difference. From that high I couldn't see that the people were all good guys. I did see a barn where I could hide if we had to bail out. Maybe there was a hayloft where some dark-eyed French girl was waiting with a couple of jugs of wine. Maybe there was a storm trooper with big boots and a bayonet to comb through the hay.

I decided to stay up high as long as possible....

"We're over Belgium," Benson called up after a while. "That big town is Brussels."

It looked peaceful down there....

Two P-51s came jazzing by, looking for game.

I traded with Sam for a while and he went on the interphone. There was nothing but shrieks with static.

Then I heard this guy call in to the wing leader. "I'm going down. Our oxygen's gone. Can you get us some escort?" He was breathing like a horse. "My navigator's shot to hell. I got to go down." There was terror in his voice.

Up there somewhere in that soft blue sky a navigator was dying. It was pretty hard to believe....

We started letting down when we crossed the coast. The formation began to loosen up a little....

At sixteen thousand I took off my helmet....I rubbed my face but it felt like a piece of fish. The candy bar tasted wonderful.

When we hit the English coast I was flying.

"Tighten it up a little," Sam said. "They said to tighten it up." He waved me in closer. "That navigator is still dying," he said thoughtfully. "That guy keeps calling in...".

I put the wheels down and Sam came in high and plunked us in halfway down the runway.

"We been to the war," Sharpe said.

"We're back now," Bird said.

D-Day and the Battle of the Bulge

The long-awaited Allied invasion of occupied France took place on June 6, 1944 after more than a year of preparation. Code-named Operation Overlord and referred to as D-Day, this cross-channel invasion was commanded by General Eisenhower who assembled nearly three million troops as well as tanks, airplanes, jeeps and other equipment in southern England.

The Germans expected an Allied invasion to open a second front, but they were unsure as to where and when it would occur. All along the beaches of northern France they placed mines, jagged wooden logs, and metal stakes to defend against the coming attack. On bluffs overlooking the beaches, the Germans positioned machine guns and mortars.

The shortest channel crossing between England and France was in the Pas de Calais and the Allies believed the Germans would expect this area to be the focus of the invasion. Instead, the Allies selected Normandy as their landing point but did everything they could to convince Hitler the invasion would take place at Calais. This included construction of a decoy army of wooden tanks, planes, and ships in the south of England, directly across from Calais, as well as phony radio messages and news reports. Hitler's intuition told him the invasion would come at Normandy. However, he did not overrule his senior commanders, who believed the invasion would come near Calais, and it was there that he sent the more experienced troops and tank forces.

The weather was poor in early June. However, a slight clearing during the early hours of the 5th made Eisenhower decide to go ahead with the invasion early on the 6th. The British Broadcasting Corporation (BBC) announced in secret code that the invasion was on, and French resistance fighters cut German communication lines all throughout Normandy. At 2 A.M. thousands of Allied paratroopers were flown over the French coast and dropped miles behind enemy lines. Their job was to take control of bridges and roads leading to the Normandy beaches after a bombardment of the area by offshore Allied guns.

The invasion began at 6:30 a.m. when American infantrymen landed on Utah and Omaha Beaches. British soldiers came ashore at Gold and Sword Beaches, and Canadians landed on Juno Beach. The Americans at Utah Beach and the British and Canadian troops were able to secure their beachheads quickly and move inland with light casualties. Apparently, the Nazis were caught off guard and still confused as to the main Allied invasion point. But the assault on Omaha Beach met stiff German resistance.

German artillery positions overlooking Omaha beach were not destroyed by Allied guns and soldiers were cut down by heavy machine gun fire before they even reached shore. Landing crafts exploded and tanks were hit. The men were pinned down at the water's edge and after an hour of experiencing heavy casualties, no advance had been made. Finally, an American destroyer, the Frankford, moved in closer to shore and began an intense bombardment of German positions. This allowed soldiers to move forward slowly so that by late afternoon Omaha Beach was secured.

On D-Day, Allied troops used specially-designed small landing craft which carried the soldiers to the beaches. Amphibious tanks rolled ashore along with projectile tanks which were able to clear away beach obstacles. After the landing, the Allies used two huge portable harbors, called mulberries, to unload additional troops and supplies, avoiding the heavy surf and rocky hazards along the beach.

There were nearly 5,000 American casualties on D-Day, but the U.S. troops, along with their British and Canadian counterparts, maintained their foothold in France. They moved slowly inland in the first stage of what was soon to become the liberation of Europe from German tyranny. Within a month, a million Allied soldiers followed. For Hitler and the Nazi cause, it was the beginning of the end.

After brutal fighting in the French countryside, the American Third Army rolled across France, liberating the coastal region of Brittany and defeating the German Seventh Army at the Battle of Falaise Gap. Paris was liberated on August 25 after the German commander, ignoring Hitler's orders to burn the famous city, surrendered to Free French troops.

The Allied armies continued their march to Germany. In the north were the British and Canadian forces. To the south, America's First, Third, and Ninth armies swept eastward. By mid-September, Belgium and Luxembourg were liberated. By the fall of 1944, the Allied offensive slowed to a halt to allow fuel and supply lines time to catch up with their tremendous advances.

Meanwhile, the Germans were being squeezed on the eastern front by the Russians, who were also on the offensive, pushing the hated enemy back at every opportunity. The Soviets relieved the city of Leningrad after an 890-day siege in which more than 500,000 people had died of starvation and exposure. Then the Russians advanced into Poland, Romania, and Bulgaria. They liberated Belgrade, Yugoslavia and entered Hungary.

It was obvious time was running out for the Third Reich, and Hitler planned one last surprise offensive against the Allies. The Ardennes Forest separated the American First and Third armies from each other and was only lightly defended since the Americans didn't expect an attack at this point.

The Germans secretly gathered together nearly 300,000 troops and 1,000 tanks, attacked through the Ardennes Forest, drove a wedge between the American armies, and recaptured the port of Antwerp in Belgium. However, Hitler underestimated the character, commitment, and determination of the Allies. He hoped they would abandon Europe after a major defeat, thus allowing him to shift all his forces to the eastern front.

The German attack (known as the Battle of the Bulge) began on December 16, 1944, and came as a complete surprise to the American forces. The Germans advanced 30 to 65 miles at various points, creating a bulge in the Allied lines. But the enemy offensive was halted when American troops, outnumbered and surrounded, managed to hold their position in the key town of Bastogne for seven days.

On December 22, when the Germans demanded a surrender, American General Anthony C. McAuliffe's reply was "Nuts!" In a race against time, Patton's Third Army broke through German lines and reached Bastogne on December 26. American counterattacks crushed the enemy forces by January 15, 1945 and drove onward into Germany itself.

With the end in sight, Hitler grew more desperate. He created a home guard of old men and young boys to defend the fatherland and ordered every German soldier to fight to the death. He ordered all German factories, farms, and bridges destroyed so the Allies would have nothing to capture. Then the Nazi leader moved into an underground bunker in Berlin and waited for a miracle.

The following excerpts focus on the D-Day invasion.

Communique No. 1 - Supreme Headquarters Allied Expeditionary Force

9:00 a.m. June 6, 1944

(Note: Copies were distributed to the troops before the invasion.)

Soldiers, Sailors and Airmen of the Allied Expeditionary Force!

You are about to embark on a Great Crusade, toward which we have striven these many months. The eyes of the world are upon you. The hopes and prayers of liberty-loving people everywhere march with you. In company with our brave Allies and brothers-in-arms on other Fronts, you will bring about the destruction of the German war machine, the elimination of Nazi tyranny over the oppressed people of Europe, and security for ourselves in a free world.

…The tide has turned! The free men of the world are marching together to victory!

I have full confidence in your courage, devotion to duty and skill in battle. We will accept nothing less than full Victory!

Good luck! And let us all beseech the blessing of Almighty God upon this great and noble undertaking.

Dwight D. Eisenhower

General Dwight D. Eisenhower gives the order "Full victory—nothing else" to paratroopers in England just before they board their planes.

The Longest Day

by Cornelius Ryan

(from Sterling, *op cit.*, pages 219, 221, 223 - 226.)

...Through the din and clamor one sound was nearer, deadlier than all the rest—the sound of machine-gun bullets clanging across the steel, snoutlike noses of the boats. Artillery roared. Mortar shells rained down. All along the four miles of Omaha Beach German guns flayed the assault craft....

They came ashore on Omaha Beach, the slogging, unglamorous men that no one envied. No battle ensigns flew for them, no horns or bugles sounded. But they had history on their side. They came from regiments that had bivouacked at places like Valley Forge, Stoney Creek, Antietam, Gettysburg, that had fought in the Argonne. They had crossed the beaches of North Africa, Sicily and Salerno. Now they had one more beach to cross. They would call this one "Bloody Omaha."

The most intense fire came from the cliffs and high bluffs at either end of the crescent-shaped beach—in the 29th Division's Dog Green area to the west and the 1st Division's Fox Green sector to the east. Here the Germans had concentrated their heaviest defenses.... Everywhere along the beach men encountered heavy fire as their boats came in, but the troops landing at Dog Green and Fox Green hadn't a chance. German gunners on the cliffs looked almost directly down on the waterlogged assault craft that heaved and pitched toward these sectors of the beach. Awkward and slow, the assault boats were nearly stationary in the water. They were sitting ducks. Coxswains at the tillers, trying desperately to maneuver their unwieldy craft through the forest of mined obstacles, now had to run the gauntlet of fire from the cliffs....

Within the first few minutes of the carnage at Dog Green one entire company was put out of action. Less than a third of the men survived the bloody walk from the boats to the edge of the beach. Their officers were killed, severely wounded or missing, and the men, weaponless and shocked, huddled at the base of the cliffs all day....

45

It was 7 A.M. The second wave of troops arrived on the shambles that was Omaha Beach. Men splashed ashore under the saturating fire of the enemy. Landing craft joined the ever-growing graveyard of wrecked, blazing hulks. Each wave of boats gave up its own bloody contribution to the incoming tide, and all along the crescent-shaped strip of beach dead Americans gently nudged each other in the water....

Into the chaos, confusion and death on the beach poured the men of the third wave—and stopped. Minutes later the fourth wave came in—and stopped. Men lay shoulder to shoulder on the sands, stones and shale. They crouched down behind obstacles; they sheltered among the bodies of the dead. Pinned down by the enemy fire which they had expected to be neutralized, confused by their landings in the wrong sectors, bewildered by the absence of the sheltering craters they had expected from the air force bombing, and shocked by the devastation and death all around them, the men froze on the beaches. They seemed in the grip of a strange paralysis....

Wounded soldiers on Omaha Beach

The shock would not last long. Even now a few men here and there, realizing that to stay on the beach meant certain death, were on their feet and moving....

Ranging up and down the 1st Division sector, oblivious to the artillery and machine-gun fire that raked the sands, was the 16th's commanding officer, Colonel George A. Taylor. "Two kinds of people are staying on this beach," he yelled, "the dead and those who are going to die. Now let's get the hell out of here."

Everywhere intrepid leaders, privates and generals alike, were showing the way, getting the men off the beach. Once started, the troops did not stop again....

★★★

David Stephen Douglass
(from Lidz, *op cit*, pages 185 - 187.)

...When we hit the water, I'd say it was chest high. We were about a hundred yards from the beach at this point, but it felt like a lot more than a hundred. The water was cold as hell and there was a lot of surf and you are loaded down with about a hundred and fifty pounds of heavy and cumbersome gear. You can barely move, and they are firing at you....There were bodies all over the place in the water, some floating face up, some face down. The first thing I did was to make for the nearest steel obstacle and hide behind it. This is what most of us did.

Some guys in the earlier waves had made it to the cover of a seawall about ten or twenty yards up on the beach. On Omaha Beach there was a kind of breakwater that provided some protection if you could get to it, but it was hard to get there. There were a lot of dead and wounded men lying on the exposed sand between the surf and the seawall. So if you were coming in from the water, you made first for the obstacles and hid behind those. Someone who hasn't been through it can't possibly imagine how exposed, how naked you feel in the face of enemy fire. Especially when it's as concentrated as it was on Omaha Beach....

It's almost impossible to give an impression of what was happening on that beach. The smell, the noise, the sense of utter and awful and total confusion, the men lying dead and wounded in the water and on the beach. Packs, ammunition, rations, boxes, communications equipment, all kinds of gear strewn all over the place. Wreckage everywhere. You just have no idea of what it was like. It was beyond imagining....

Finally, some of our destroyers came very close inshore, began firing very accurately on the German positions, and knocked a number of them out. It's much easier to hit a gun position when you can see it firing. During our softening up bombardment the Germans hadn't returned our fire, so the Navy had a hard time getting an accurate fix on them. But now, with the German guns blazing away, our spotters could fix the German positions exactly....

As the balance of firepower began to shift in our favor, more and more German positions were knocked out. They lost the advantage of being able to blanket all areas of the beach with crossfire. From then on we took one position after another, either by flanking or by frontal assault. The bulldozer tanks helped cut paths through the wire and the minefields and by mid-afternoon all resistance on Omaha had ceased....

★ ★ ★

Normandy Beach

France: June 1944—September 1944
by Ernie Pyle

(from Pyle, *op cit.*, pages 280 -282, 351-352, 354.)

NORMANDY BEACHHEAD, June 16, 1944—

...The wreckage was vast and startling. The awful waste and destruction of war, even aside from the loss of human life, has always been one of its outstanding features to those who are in it. Anything and everything is expendable. And we did expend on our beachhead in Normandy during those first few hours.

A few hundred yards back on the beach is a high bluff. Up there we had a tent hospital and a barbed-wire enclosure for prisoners of war. From up there you could see far up and down the beach, in a spectacular crow's-nest view, and far out to sea.

And standing out there on the water beyond all this wreckage was the greatest armada man has ever seen. You simply could not believe the gigantic collection of ships that lay out there waiting to unload....

As I stood up there I noticed a group of freshly taken German prisoners standing nearby. They had not yet been put in the prison cage. They were just standing there, a couple of doughboys leisurely guarding them with tommy guns.

The prisoners too were looking out to sea—the same bit of sea that for months and years had been so safely empty before their gaze. Now they stood staring almost as if in a trance.

They didn't say a word to each other. They didn't need to. The expression on their faces was something forever unforgettable. In it was the final horrified acceptance of their doom....

U.S. troops under fire storming the beach on D-Day.

The Liberation of Paris

PARIS, August 28, 1944 —

I had thought that for me there could never again be any elation in war. But I had reckoned without the liberation of Paris—I had reckoned without remembering that I might be a part of this richly historic day....

The streets were lined as by Fourth of July parade crowds at home, only this crowd was almost hysterical. The streets of Paris are very wide, and they were packed on each side. The women were all brightly dressed in white or red blouses and colorful peasant skirts, with flowers in their hair and big flashy earrings. Everybody was throwing flowers....

As our jeep eased through the crowds, thousands of people crowded up, leaving only a narrow corridor, and frantic men, women and children grabbed us and kissed us and shook our hands and beat on our shoulders and slapped our backs and shouted their joy as we passed.

...We got kissed until we were literally red in face, and I must say we enjoyed it....

Of all the days of national joy I've ever witnessed this is the biggest...

Airmen returning to the U.S. from an overseas flight on their bomber, "Hell Hen."

The End of the War

Allied forces began their final advance into Germany in the winter of 1945. In the east, the Soviet armies drove westward through Austria and Czechoslovakia and across the Vistula River into Germany. In the west, American forces took Cologne and then crossed the Rhine when Germans failed to destroy a bridge at Remagen. The First, Third, and Ninth armies pushed rapidly through Central Germany.

By the beginning of April, a combined British-American force surrounded the industrial Ruhr Valley and overwhelmed any German resistance. When Russian and American troops met at the Elbe River several weeks later, the German forces were cut in half.

A decision was made by General Eisenhower to halt the eastward march of the western allies and allow the Russians to take Berlin. The battle of Berlin became the last major offensive of the war in Europe.

While the western Allies advanced north and south of the German capital, eliminating pockets of enemy resistance, Russian troops left a destructive and bloody trail in their wake as they marched toward the heart of the Nazi empire. Eager to take revenge on the Germans who had slaughtered so many of their countrymen, the Russians brutally brought the reality of the war home to the German people who had so loyally supported their Fuehrer. A force of nearly three million troops, 6,250 armored vehicles, and 7,500 aircraft encircled the city. With a cry of "two eyes for every eye," the Russians engaged in ferocious street fighting in apartment buildings, parks, stores, and even the Berlin Zoo.

By April 30 the Russians controlled the city and Adolf Hitler committed suicide in his underground bunker. German forces throughout Europe, who had stubbornly continued to resist the Allies, finally surrendered in defeat. On May 7, 1945, the unconditional surrender of Germany was officially signed by General Alfred Jodl at Eisenhower's headquarters at Reims and all fighting ended.

American President Franklin Roosevelt had died on April 12, and his successor, Harry S. Truman, took up the reins of power and completed the task begun by FDR years before. Truman declared

May 8 as Victory in Europe Day (V-E Day), then turned his attention to ending the war in the Pacific.

The following excerpts focus on the Allied drive into Germany, the battle of Berlin, and the end of the war.

Americans Risk Lives

by Howard Cowan

(*The New York Times*, March 9, 1945.)

ON THE RHINE BRIDGEHEAD, March 9 —

One of the great dramatic moments of the war occurred late Wednesday when a nerveless band of Americans jerked loose the wires attached to tons of German-set explosives. Lieut. John Mitchell of Pittsburgh, Pa., found the cache of explosives and directed the disconnection of the wires.

Only one-way traffic was possible over the bridge for several hours, but engineers, working under fire, then repaired the slight damage to its surface and released the full torrent of men and machines.

Some tank crews, too impatient to wait, trained their guns across the river and blasted the Germans on the east bank from the streets of Remagen. Field guns hastily wheeled to the west bank also joined in throwing a sheet of fire across to protect the bridge, and the terror-stricken residents of Remagen fled to the fields behind the town.

So stunned were the Germans by the act of the Americans in dashing onto the explosive-laden structure that two prisoners actually were taken on the bridge itself. Within two hours hundreds of other prisoners were laying down their arms and confusing the situation on the east bank.

The inhabitants of Erfel on the east bank, believing they were secure behind the great Rhine moat, had made no move to evacuate, but they quickly produced white flags and set them flapping from the buildings....

Road to Berlin

by Hal Boyle

(Associated Press, March 27, 1945.)

This is the greatest armored joyride in history—and Adolf Hitler literally paved the way for his own downfall. The great single- and double-lane highways he built in peace to shuttle his armies out from the heart of Germany to attack neighboring countries are proving his undoing.

They are smooth concrete avenues to Berlin and other great German cities over which the mightiest masses of armor ever assembled in the west are now rolling at true blitzkrieg pace in a dozen columns, coming from so many directions the Germans are powerless to scrape together enough troops to halt them all....

Minefields, road blocks and antitank guns slow these giant columns only momentarily. Doughboys leap from the iron tanks and sweep in from the flanks to drive away or kill the enemy antitank gunners with rifle fire. Bulldozers move up in front of the column under cover of protecting tank guns and shove aside road-blocking debris from blown bridges and overhead spans as combat engineers sweep a path through the minefields. Then the column smashes forward again at full speed....

They have swept through some towns so fast the householders hadn't time to put up white flags of surrender and the surprised Nazi garrisons were caught outside their positions, their guns unmanned. After a few minutes shelling they give up readily and infantry units then move in to clean out the snipers.

No attempt is being made to save Nazi real estate. Whenever the tankmen suspect a building or home may house a German strongpoint, they blow it apart and race by.

"When in doubt—fire first," is their motto....

Berlin—Broken Skeleton of a City

by Ernest Leiser

(*Stars and Stripes*, Paris Edition, May 10, 1945)

BERLIN, May 5 (Delayed)—Berlin, the capital of defeat, today is a charred, stinking, broken skeleton of a city.

It is impossible to imagine what it looked like before. It is impossible to believe that the miles of disembowelled buildings, of cratered streets, of shattered masonry once could have been the capital of Greater Germany and the home of 4,000,000 people.

Only a handful of those 4,000,000 still remain as the last clatter of machine-gun fire echoes through the hollow city. There are no factories left for them to work in, no shops, no theatres, no office buildings.

But the handful are busy today: They are shovelling the rubble from the streets, sweeping the dead out of the way—working while the Russian conquerors still walk the streets with straggling columns of prisoners or wander around staring at the shells of once-great buildings of state. They are working, oblivious of the light, chill rain that is the only mourning for the death of their homes....

Thus it is with the German capital today, two days after its official capture by the Russians. Street fights are just coming to an end, and the smell of sewage and death is everywhere. It is one great tombstone....

The War in Europe is Ended!
Surrender is Unconditional

by Edward Kennedy

(*The New York Times*, May 8, 1945)

REIMS, FRANCE, May 7—Germany surrendered unconditionally to the Western Allies and the Soviet Union at 2:41 A.M. French time today. [This was at 8:41 P.M. Eastern war time, Sunday, May 6, 1945.]

The surrender took place at a little red schoolhouse that is the headquarters of General Dwight D. Eisenhower....

General Eisenhower was not present at the signing, but immediately afterward General Jodl and his fellow delegate, General Admiral Hans Georg Friedeburg, were received by the Supreme Commander.

They were asked sternly if they understood the surrender terms imposed upon Germany and if they would be carried out by Germany.

They answered yes.

Germany, which began the war with a ruthless attack upon Poland, followed by successive aggressions and brutality in concentration camps, surrendered with an appeal to the victors for mercy toward the German people and armed forces....

German officers signing Germany's surrender on May 7, 1945.

CBS Broadcast by Charles Collingwood
May 8, 1945

Germany surrendered at 2:45 on the morning of May 7, 1945. At that moment, General Jodl, Chief of Staff of the German Army, signed the last document....

It was all over—the Germans had surrendered—and later General Eisenhower said a few words. This is what he said: "...The Allied force, which invaded Europe on June 6, 1944, has, with its great Russian ally, and forces advancing in the south, utterly defeated the Germans by land, sea and air. Thus, unconditional surrender has been achieved by teamwork, teamwork not only among all the Allies participating but amongst all the services—land, sea and air. To every subordinate that has been in this command, of almost five million Allies, I owe a debt of gratitude that can never be repaid. The only repayment that can be made to them is the deep appreciation and lasting gratitude of all free citizens of all the United Nations."

...The most terrible war in human history had finally come to an end. The mad dog of Europe was put out of the way, the strange, insane monstrosity that was Nazi Germany had been beaten into submission....

Thousands of troops came home
on the Queen Mary

The GI

by Sgt. Debs Myers

(*Yank Magazine*, Various Editions, 1945, from *Yank--The Army Weekly*, Steve Kluger, New York: St. Martin's Press, 1991, page 349.)

The civilian...became a soldier.

He learned how to sleep in the mud, tie a knot, kill a man.

He learned the ache of loneliness, the ache of exhaustion, the kinship of misery. From the beginning he wanted to go home. He learned that men make the same queasy noises in the morning, feel the same longings at night; that every man is alike and that each man is different....

He was often bored; he wasn't always brave; most times he was scared....

The GI did not destroy fascism. But he helped defeat the fascists and he took away their guns.

He was part of an army that left its bootprints on three continents....With his allies he saved the world; and hoped to God he'd never have to do it again.

He had learned the ache of loneliness, the ache of exhaustion, the kinship of misery. He had learned how to sleep in the mud, tie a knot, kill a man.

And having learned all this, if he got through all right, the soldier came home and...became a civilian.

Crimes against Humanity

Adolf Hitler's belief that Aryans were the true "master race" and his intense hatred of the Jewish people were part of the basic foundation of Nazi ideology. The Nazis were able to carry out their war against the Jews with minimal civilian interference. The historical German anti-semitism allowed most people to ignore what was happening to their neighbors without feeling guilty. Thus, it was not difficult for the Nazis to progress from prohibiting Jews from holding certain jobs and beating them in the streets, to sending them to concentration camps where systematic mass murder was carried out.

The details of Nazi horrors were only made public in the last months of the war when American and Soviet troops liberated prisoners in Belsen, Buchenwald, Dachau, Auschwitz, Treblinka, and other death camps throughout Europe.

General Dwight Eisenhower, shocked at the numbers of living skeletons and stacks of dead bodies in the camps, ordered American soldiers to tour the area so they would understand the evils of Nazism they were fighting against. Then he forced German civilians who lived in the vicinity to see firsthand what they had always chosen to ignore.

Forty percent of the world's Jewish population (six million) had been murdered by the Nazis, as well as five million gypsies, Slavs, Poles, homosexuals, political prisoners, the mentally deficient, and other non-Aryans. Yet, not all non-Jews turned their backs on their fellow man. Thousands saved Jews (and others) from death and deportation at the risk of their own lives and have been honored in Israel as the "Righteous among the Nations."

The war crimes trials held at Nuremberg, Germany between November 1945 and October 1946 revealed, through film, documents, and testimony, the full extent of Nazi atrocities to the world. Among the 22 on trial, 12 were sentenced to death, seven to prison, and three were acquitted.

The terrible crimes committed in the name of racial purity have led all people of conscience to vow that "never again" should such acts of hatred and prejudice be ignored or tolerated against any race, religion, or group of people.

Survivors of Buchenwald concentration camp were liberated by U.S. troops in April 1945.

Aftermath

Peace had finally descended over war-torn Europe. Many of its once beautiful cities lay in ruins. The picturesque countryside, pockmarked by bomb craters, was now a graveyard for destroyed tanks and trucks. Whole towns no longer existed.

The glorious plans for Hitler's world empire lay buried beneath the rubble along with his remains. The Allies had joined together to defeat the fanatical evil dictator whose aim was to enslave the world. They succeeded—but at a great cost in human lives and mass destruction. As many as 35 million (including military and civilians) died in the war against Germany. Millions were left homeless. The Jewish people were almost totally eliminated from the European continent in the Nazi holocaust.

America's arsenal produced the supplies, equipment, ships, tanks, and guns that turned the tide against the Germans. Allied troops—including the "Greatest Generation" of American soldiers—did their duty with courage and honor as they fought their way across Europe.

Adolf Hitler could never understand that a free people working by choice could out-produce any slave labor force deprived of liberty and dignity. In World War II, America's factory workers—including women who filled jobs made vacant when men left to serve in the military—were just as important as its front line soldiers.

What emerged from postwar Europe was a world now dominated by the two major powers who had done so much to defeat Hitler. After the Soviets drove westward into Germany in the final offensive of the war, rather than giving up their authority in the areas they liberated from fascist oppression, they consolidated it. Stalin imposed communist puppet governments in Poland, Romania, Bulgaria, Czechoslovakia, and other eastern European nations, all controlled by Moscow.

At first, Germany was divided into sections controlled by the major Allies: the United States, Great Britain, France, and the Soviet Union. By 1949, Germany was divided into two states. The Federal Republic (West Germany) became a free democratic society with a capitalist free market economy while the German Democratic Republic (East Germany) was quickly dominated by Soviet communism.

The mounting tension between the communist and non-communist countries soon escalated into what was referred to as the "Cold War." It was Winston Churchill who said in 1946 that "...an iron curtain has descended across the [European] Continent." The terms "cold war" and "iron curtain" were key phrases used to describe the volatile political situation with the Soviets.

This communist versus capitalist mentality dominated the world scene for more than 40 years, fueled by the possibility of a nuclear war brought on by the stockpiling of atomic weapons on both sides. It was not until after 1989, with the fall of communism, the reunification of Germany, and the breakup of the Soviet Union, that the Cold War ended.

Some historians have referred to World War II as "the last good war," though many believe that no war could possibly be good. Yet the Second World War was a conflict in which good and evil were clearly delineated, with the allies in combat against the worst of human brutality.

Although the fighting in the Pacific did not end for several more months and despite the emerging, awful details of the Holocaust, a measure of relief was felt in Europe and the United States after the war in Europe had ended and freedom had triumphed over fascism.

On a Note of Triumph

by Norman Corwin

(CBS Broadcast, April, 1945)

> ...what do we know now
> that we didn't know before?
> What have we LEARNED out of this war?...

WE'VE LEARNED THAT NATIONS WHICH DON'T KNOW WHAT THEY WANT WILL GET WHAT THEY DON'T WANT....

WE'VE LEARNED THAT SOME MEN WILL FIGHT FOR POWER, BUT THAT MOST MEN WILL FIGHT TO BE FREE.

WE'VE LEARNED THAT FREEDOM ISN'T SOMETHING TO BE WON AND THEN FORGOTTEN. IT MUST BE RENEWED, LIKE SOIL AFTER YIELDING GOOD CROPS; MUST BE REWOUND, LIKE A FAITHFUL CLOCK; EXERCISED, LIKE A HEALTHY MUSCLE....